BY Toni Buzzeo

ILLUSTRATED BY Diana Sudyka

WHEN SUE FOUND SUE

Sue Hendrickson Discovers Her T. Rex

ABRAMS BOOKS FOR YOUNG READERS · NEW YORK

For Sue Hendrickson and all of the
curious women finders
—T. B.

For Isabel: The world is illuminated by your curiosity
—D. S.

This book was created with gouache and watercolors made from
earth pigments for the Dakota scenes.

Library of Congress Cataloging-in-Publication Data

Names: Buzzeo, Toni, author. | Sudyka, Diana, illustrator.
Title: When Sue found Sue: Sue Hendrickson discovers her T. rex /
by Toni Buzzeo; illustrated by Diana Sudyka.
Other titles: Sue Hendrickson and Sue, the T. rex
Description: New York: Abrams Books for Young Readers, 2019.
Identifiers: LCCN 2017054249 | ISBN 9781419731631 (hardcover with jacket)
Subjects: LCSH: Hendrickson, Sue, 1949—Juvenile literature. | Sue
(Tyrannosaurus rex)—Juvenile literature. | Paleontologists—United
States—Biography. | Women paleontologists—United States—Biography. |

Tyrannosaurus rex—Juvenile literature.

Classification: LCC QE707.H46 B89 2019 | DDC 560/.92 [B]—dc23

Text copyright © 2019 Toni Buzzeo
Illustrations copyright © 2019 Diana Sudyka
Book design by Pamela Notarantonio

Printed and bound in China
10 9 8 7 6 5 4 3 2 1

Abrams Books for Young Readers are available at special discounts when
purchased in quantity for premiums and promotions as well as fundraising or
educational use. Special editions can also be created to specification.
For details, contact specialsales@abramsbooks.com or the address below.

Abrams® is a registered trademark of Harry N. Abrams, Inc.

ABRAMS The Art of Books
195 Broadway, New York, NY 10007
abramsbooks.com

"Never lose your curiosity about everything
in the universe—
it can take you to places you never
thought possible!"

—SUE HENDRICKSON

Sue Hendrickson was born to *find things*:
missing trinkets,
prehistoric butterflies,
sunken ships,
even buried dinosaurs.

If it was lost, Sue's curiosity
led her on a hunt to find it.

Sue began searching for lost treasure
when she was mighty small.
She was born shy and incredibly smart.
Treasure hunting was
the perfect job for a shy girl.
When she was young,
Sue would walk alone through the alley
behind her home in Munster, Indiana,
with her head down.
She was on a mission—
to *find things*!

And she often did,
like the little brass perfume bottle
she's never lost.

Sue wasn't like other kids.
So shy and smart,
Sue gobbled up books
the way other kids gobbled up gingersnaps.
Head down, a book a day,
Sue learned things all on her own.

She dialed her curiosity up to HIGH
and discovered everything
about anything that interested her.

Sue's curiosity led her to visit
The Field Museum of Natural History in Chicago.
She loved to view
the endless supply of treasures
that other hunters—
maybe shy outsiders themselves—
had already found.

HADROSAURUS

TRICERATOPS

Sue couldn't wait to grow up
and search the wide world
for hidden treasure on her own.

At the age of seventeen,
Sue launched her life of discovery—
traveling, living outdoors, supporting herself,
and *finding things*!
One curiosity always led to another.
And for the first time, Sue joined teams—
teams of curious, dedicated treasure hunters.

Diving first for tropical fish,
and then for lost boats,
lost airplanes, and even lost cars,
eventually led Sue
to search Dominican amber mines
        for extinct prehistoric butterflies,
to search the deserts of Peru
        for prehistoric-whale fossils,
and finally—FINALLY!—
to search the hills of western South Dakota
        for dinosaur fossils.

For four long, hot, dusty summers,
Sue dug for duck-billed dino fossils—
taking down the big rocks
with a shovel and pick,
then freeing the bones,
      first with a rock hammer,
      then with a digging knife,
      then with an X-ACTO knife and a tiny pick,
      and finally dusting the area with a paintbrush
      to remove all traces of rock from the bone.

No showers for washing,
no beds for sleeping,
no escape from the beating sun,
but still, Sue was part of a team.
She loved the work, the discovery, and
the chance to be curious and *find things*.

During the last weeks
of her fourth summer of digging for duckbills
in the blistering heat,
Sue Hendrickson felt pulled
to a sandstone cliff
far off in the distance.
She couldn't say why then—
and she can't say why even now—
but she was called to that cliff.
And on August 12, 1990,
when her team headed into town
to fix a flat tire,
Sue finally followed her curiosity.

She and her golden retriever, Gypsy,
left camp alone that morning in a dense, misty fog—
so unusual in the hot, dry plains.
They hiked for four hours
across seven miles of rugged prairie land
before they finally reached the rock face
Sue had been so curious about.

Sue and Gypsy stood below
the sixty-foot-high towering cliff
of tan and gray rock.

"I walked around the base of the cliff
with my head down, watching the ground.
About halfway along,
I noticed a few pieces of what looked like bones.
Then I looked up."

Sue stared up at three enormous backbones
protruding from the cliff
eight feet above her.
She felt a thrill run through her.
Could it be?
It was hard to believe,
but Sue knew by their incredible size
what those fossils must be—
a Tyrannosaurus rex!

"I could see them quite clearly
in the sunlight,
as though waiting patiently
for someone to find them."
Once again, Sue Hendrickson did
what a shy outsider girl
had trained herself to do so well—
she *found* them!

Sue rushed back to the campsite,
humming with
        the excitement,
        the happiness, and
        the thrill of her find.
She couldn't wait to tell the others.

A Tyrannosaurus rex!

Her team immediately named the dinosaur
Sue the T. rex
after Sue Hendrickson, the finder.
Then they raced to free the T. rex
from her cliff.

But releasing three hundred T. rex bones
in 115-degree heat
under the sweltering sun
without damaging the bones
was neither quick nor easy.

For five days, Sue and the team
worked from sunrise to sunset,
breaking rocks with picks
and digging with shovels to remove nearly
thirty feet of sandstone and hard soil.

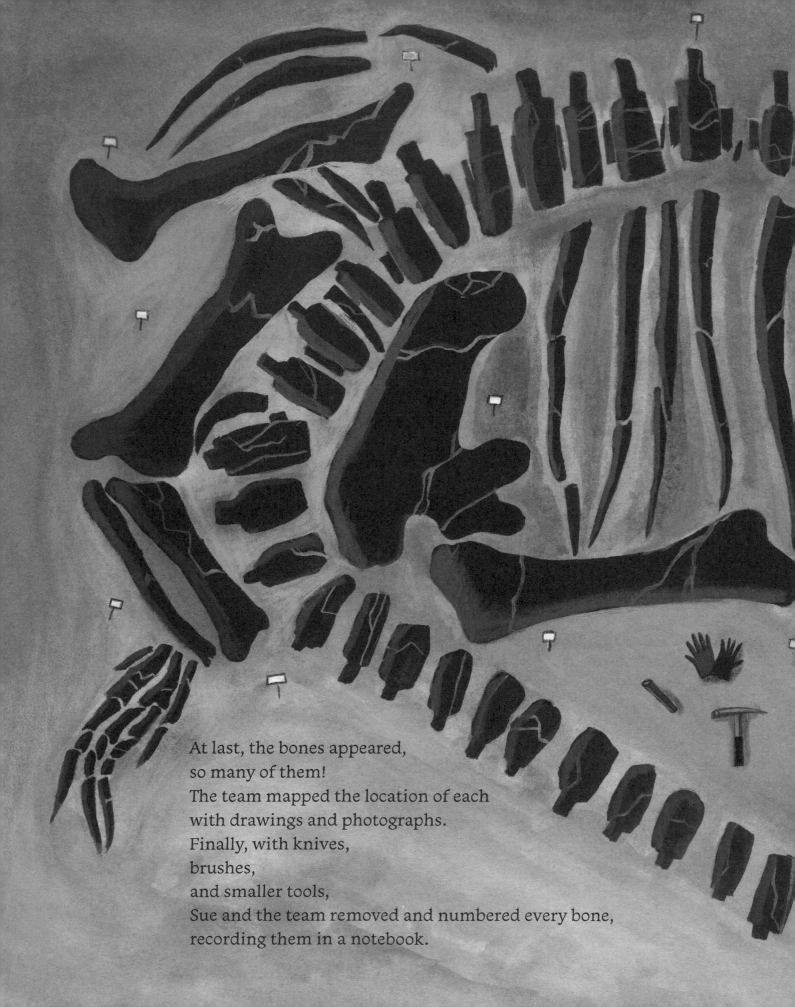

At last, the bones appeared,
so many of them!
The team mapped the location of each
with drawings and photographs.
Finally, with knives,
brushes,
and smaller tools,
Sue and the team removed and numbered every bone,
recording them in a notebook.

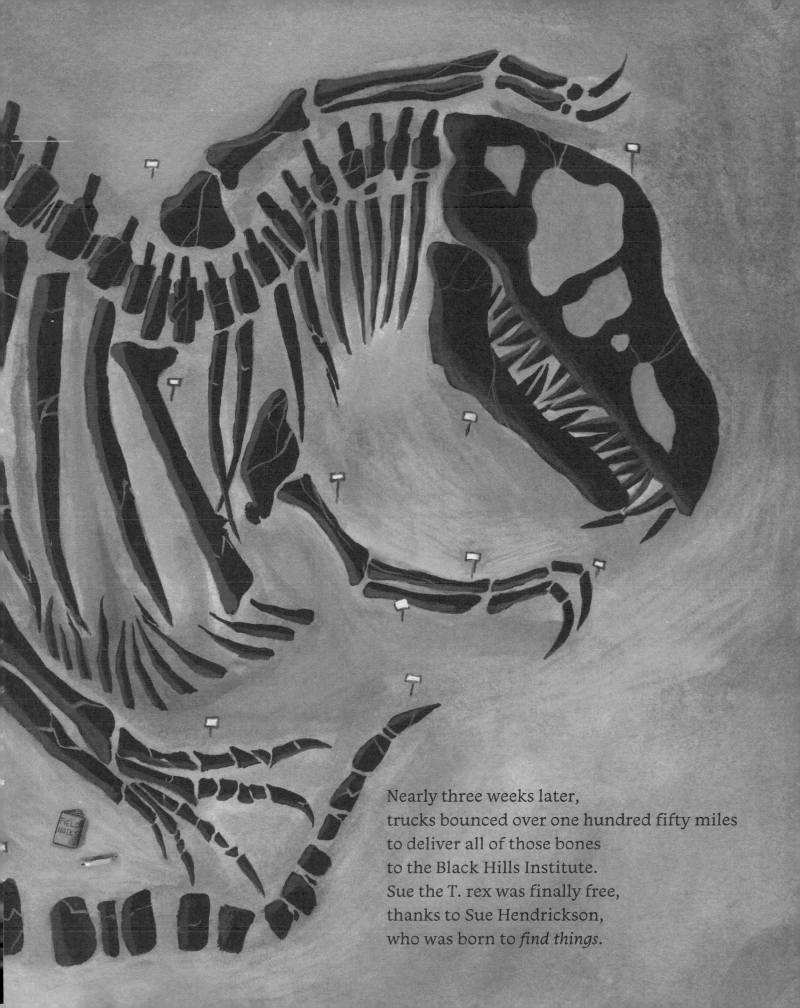

Nearly three weeks later,
trucks bounced over one hundred fifty miles
to deliver all of those bones
to the Black Hills Institute.
Sue the T. rex was finally free,
thanks to Sue Hendrickson,
who was born to *find things*.

After a long dispute about ownership,
Sue the T. rex went to auction.
And who won the auction?
None other than The Field Museum—
the very same museum Sue Hendrickson
loved to visit so often as a young girl.

SUE
TYRANNOSAURUS REX

Walk into The Field Museum of Natural History in Chicago.
Inside, Sue the T. rex towers over you.
She is the world's largest,
most complete,
best-preserved
Tyrannosaurus rex fossil
discovered so far.

And she was found by Sue Hendrickson,
that once-shy girl,
so different from the others,
whose curiosity
has always led her to *find things*—
and always will.

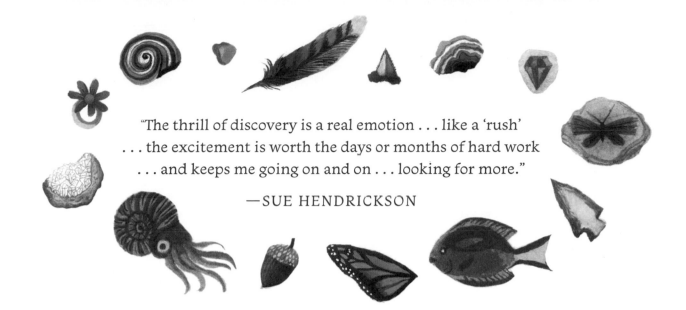

"The thrill of discovery is a real emotion . . . like a 'rush'
. . . the excitement is worth the days or months of hard work
. . . and keeps me going on and on . . . looking for more."

—SUE HENDRICKSON

AUTHOR'S NOTE

IMAGINE someone who is an adventurer, an explorer, an underwater archaeological excavation diver, a marine archaeologist, a dinosaur hunter, a field paleontologist, and a renowned expert on amber fossils. Meet Sue Hendrickson! She is a self-educated woman of science, an explorer and treasure hunter, a seeker, and a finder. Born on December 2, 1949, in Chicago, Illinois, Sue grew up in Munster, Indiana, as a shy child and a voracious reader who was always on the lookout for treasures.

She is best known as the woman who found Sue the T. rex. Ninety years after the first T. rex skeleton was found in 1900, Sue Hendrickson found the skeleton that became known as Sue. While many other T. rexes are represented by a few important bones, Sue the T. rex is more than 90 percent complete. She's the largest (thirteen feet tall at the hip and forty-two feet long), most complete, and best-preserved T. rex ever found. What's more, when she was found, her bones were in excellent condition, rather than the fragile state in which many fossilized bones are recovered.

Unfortunately, Sue Hendrickson's great find was followed by a long and bitter dispute among various people who believed they owned Sue: Maurice Williams, the Sioux tribal member who owned the land where Sue was found; the Cheyenne River Sioux tribe on whose reservation Sue was found; the federal government that held the land in trust where Sue was found; and, of course, Peter Larson, whose Black Hills Institute team was responsible for the dig that found Sue. Only Sue Hendrickson didn't believe she owned Sue.

Perhaps this is because Sue Hendrickson is much more than the woman who found Sue the T. rex. She has been a professional diver since 1971, a specialist in paleontology fieldwork (especially dinosaurs), a specialist in fossil inclusions in amber from mines in the Dominican Republic and Mexico, and a long-standing member of the Franck Goddio marine archaeology team. Sue holds an Honorary PhD from the University of Illinois at Chicago (2000) and a Medal of Honor from Barnard College (2002).

RESOURCES FOR CHILDREN

Gaines, Ann. *Sue Hendrickson: Explorer on Land and Sea*. Philadelphia: Chelsea House, 2004.

Hendrickson, Sue. *My Life as an Explorer*. New York: Cartwheel Books, 2001.

Lunis, Natalie. *A T. Rex Named Sue: Sue Hendrickson's Huge Discovery*. New York: Bearport, 2007.

"Meet Dinosaur Expert Sue Hendrickson." Scholastic.
www.scholastic.com/teachers/article/meet-dinosaur-expert-sue-hendrickson.

Passero, Kathy. "Sue Hendrickson, A Real-Life Indiana Jones." *Biography* 4, no. 11 (November 2000).

Relf, Pat. *A Dinosaur Named Sue: The Story of the Colossal Fossil*. New York: Scholastic, 2000.

Scholastic Teacher's Activity Guide. "Ask a Dinosaur Expert." Scholastic. teacher.scholastic.com
/activities/dinosaurs/expert/transcript.htm.

Upadhyay, Ritu. "Meet a Bone-ified Explorer." *Time for Kids*, March 2, 2001.

Photo Credit: Field Museum Library/ Premium Archive/ Getty Images

ADDITIONAL SOURCES

Doubilet, Anne L. "Beneath the Sands of Time: Explorations with Sue Hendrickson." *Explorer's Journal*
(Spring 2007). backup.explorers.org/journal/spring07/beneath_the_sands_of_time.php.

Fiffer, Steve. "Indiana Bones." *Chicago Tribune*, April 4, 1999.

———.*Tyrannosaurus Sue: The Extraordinary Saga of the Largest, Most Fought over T. Rex Ever Found*. New
York: W. H. Freeman, 2000.

Hendrickson, Sue. *Sue Hendrickson*. www.sue-hendrickson.info.

Miller, Todd Douglas, dir. *Dinosaur 13*. Lionsgate, 2014.

All quotes taken from Sue Hendrickson's official website: www.sue-hendrickson.info.